YE GREAT JOKE COMPETITION

We promise that whosoever produces a JOKE that King BORIS can understand will win the VERY SPECIAL PRIZE of:...

ONE FREE ROCK for every day of their life (plus 35 pebbles if they reply within 14 days)

~ Also ~

there are 3 second prizes of a slightly smaller rock on alternate Thursdays, and 10 runners-up prizes of a bucket of GRIT, to be shared equally among the lucky winners.

YE GREAT JOKE COMPETITION

DAVID FARRIS

Hippo Books
Scholastic Publications Limited
London

Scholastic Publications Ltd,
10 Earlham Street, London WC2H 9RX, UK

Scholastic Inc,
730 Broadway, New York, NY 10003, USA

Scholastic Canada Ltd,
123 Newkirk Road, Richmond Hill,
Ontario L4C 3G5, Canada

Ashton Scholastic Pty Ltd,
P O Box 579, Gosford, New South Wales,
Australia

Ashton Scholastic Pty Ltd,
165 Marua Road, Panmure, Auckland 6,
New Zealand

First published 1990

Text and illustrations copyright © David Farris

ISBN 0 590 76355 5

Made and printed by Cox & Wyman Ltd, Reading, Berks
Typeset by AKM Associates (UK) Ltd, Southall, London

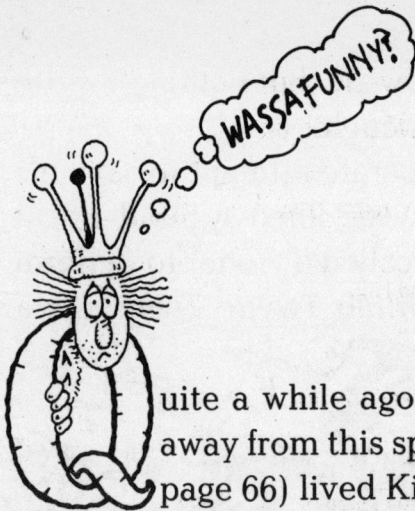

WASSA FUNNY?

uite a while ago, in a land not far away from this spot: • (see map on page 66) lived King Boris the Bamboozled, in his family home, Crumblyn Castle.

Poor King Boris could never understand a joke, no matter how simple. For many years he employed the funniest man in the land, Tyrone Twytte, to be his jester. But, although most people were thrown into fits of delirious laughter at the merest glimpse of him, Twytte couldn't raise even the slightest chuckle from the King.

While telling jokes, Twytte had been known to fall down holes, slip on banana skins, wear a large red nose, walk into walls, dress as a pantomime chicken, and once he had even dived into a giant custard pie from the top of the tallest tower in Crumblyn Castle wearing only a revolving bow-tie. But nothing Twytte did made the King laugh.

Finally, in a desperate attempt to save his reputation, Twytte was joined by his identical twin brother (also called Tyrone) to perform as *The Twiffic Twirling Twytte Twins*. As a

stage prop they used a large door with an enormous knocker on it. The brothers stood on either side of the door, both dressed in over-sized jesters' outfits, and spun round and round on the spot whilst acting out their extensive collection of Knock Knock jokes.

Knock knock!
Who's there?
Snow.
Snow who?
Snow good . . . I can't remember . . .

Knock knock!
Who's there?
Eddie.
Eddie who?
Eddie body in there?

Knock knock!
Who's there?
Dwayne.
Dwayne who?
Dwayne the bath, I'm dwowning.

Knock knock!
Who's there?
Thumping.
Thumping who?
Thumping green and hairy is crawling up my leg!

Knock knock!
Who's there?
Will.
Will who?
Will you kindly open this door?

Knock knock!
Who's there?
Fanny.
Fanny who?
Fanny how everyone keeps asking who's there . . .

Knock knock!
Who's there?
Egon.
Egon who?
Egon toast.

Knock knock!
Who's there?
Ally.
Ally who?
Ally looyah! Someone's answered the door!

Knock knock!
Who's there?
The Invisible Man.
Tell him I can't see him!

Knock knock!
Who's there?
Noah.
Noah who?
Noah good place to eat?

Knock knock!
Who's there?
Sharon.
Sharon who?
Sharon share alike.

Knock knock!
Who's there?
Oliver.
Oliver who?
Oliver lot to say when you open this door.

Knock knock!
Who's there?
Hugh Goaner.
Hugh Goaner who?
Hugh Goaner be in there long?

Knock knock!
Who's there?
Ivan.
Ivan who?
Ivan important message! Open up!

Knock knock!
Who's there?
Fozzie.
Fozzie who?
Fozzie last time, open this door!

Knock knock!
Who's there?
Lettuce.
Lettuce who?
Lettuce in, it's freezing out here!

Knock knock!
Who's there?
Noise.
Noise who?
Noise to see you again.

//.

But as their show drew to a close, King Boris just shook his head slowly. His miserable face was as miserable as ever.

On one particularly bamboozling day, the King decided to send out a Decree (in fact, he didn't really know what a decree was, so he sent it out in centigrade and Fahrenheit, just to be on the safe side). This is what it said:

We promise that whosoever produces a JOKE that King BORIS can understand will win the VERY SPECIAL PRIZE of:...
ONE FREE ROCK, for every day of their life (plus 35 pebbles if they reply within 14 days)
~ Also ~
there are 3 second prizes of a slightly smaller rock on alternate Thursdays, and 10 runners-up prizes of a bucket of GRIT, to be shared equally among the lucky winners.

Well, of course, the jokes came in from far and wide, and near and thin. One even came in from King Derek the Almost Equally Bamboozled (no relation), although his entry turned out to be a shopping list, and he had to be disqualified.

KING DEREK
(recent portrait)

The jokes were sifted and checked for rib-tickleability in the Great Crumblyn Hall, under the watchful eye of the King's personal secretary and ping-pong partner, Sir Myles of Tarmac. A troup of courtiers was specially trained to spot even the shortest jokes at a distance of 2.25 metres.

The whole castle was a bus

THAT SHOULD READ "ABUZZ"!

CLEVER KNOW-ALL

with the excitement of the challenge, even
down in the dark, damp dungeon, where Wild
'n' Wicked Wilf, the unsuccessful Chain Mail
Train robber was kept. He had amassed a

JAILOR, JAILOR! THIS BOWL
IS WET!

that's your soup!

TODAY'S
MENU

Soot
Soup

large collection of Jailor jokes to keep himself entertained during the long winter evenings, and his voice could often be heard echoing up the narrow spiralling steps as he recited the jokes to himself.

Jailor, jailor! There's a dead beetle in this soup!
Yes, they're not very good swimmers are they?

Jailor, jailor! What's this bug doing in the soup?
I think it's drowning.

Jailor, jailor! Why is this food all mashed up?
Because you asked me to step on it.

Jailor, jailor! There's a rat in my soup.
Well you did ask for something with a bit of body in it.

Jailor, jailor! You've got your sleeve in my soup.
It's all right. There's no arm in it.

Jailor, jailor! There's a fly in my soup.
It's the rotting meat that attracts them.

Jailor, jailor! There's a cockroach in this soup!
Well, that's better than no meat at all, isn't it?

Jailor, jailor! What's the meaning of this fly in my soup?
I really don't know! I don't tell fortunes!

Jailor, jailor! There's a button on my potato!
That's because it's a jacket potato!

In the Great Crumblyn Kitchens, even the preparations for the Ridiculously Huge Bread-pudding-Baking Festival came to a halt. The Royal Cook, Ivor Toastrack was concentrating so hard on inventing the wittiest joke in the Kingdom, that he forgot he was stirring a thick sticky breadpudding mix with his giant spoon, and fell into the mixture. His two assistants came to his rescue in a small boat. They then had to hurriedly chisel off the drying mix before it set with Ivor inside it.

What do you get if you cross a cow with a mule?
Milk with a kick in it.

What's orange and round and weighs 30 kilos?
A plumpkin.

What do you get if you cross rabbits with leeks?
Bunions.

Why did the banana go out with the fig?
Because it couldn't get a date.

What do you get if you cross a cow with a duck?
Cream Quackers.

Why do bananas use suntan lotion?
Because they peel.

What's the difference between a mouldy lettuce
and a miserable song?
One's a bad salad, and the other's a sad ballad.

What is rhubarb?
Celery with high blood pressure.

What's green and white and bounces?
A spring onion.

How do you make an apple puff?
Chase it round the kitchen.

What's long, green and always points north?
A magnetic cucumber.

What did the man say who had jelly and custard in
his ears?
Speak up! I'm a trifle deaf!

Knock knock!
Who's there?
Cook.
Cook who?
That's the first one I've heard this year!

Why was the cook so cross?
He had a chip on his shoulder.

What's long and green and red all over?
A cucumber holding its breath.

What's round and white and chuckles?
A tickled onion.

lsewhere in the Kingdom, the joke competition was already causing a bit of a stir. Out on the jousting green, the King's Champion, Sir Guy de Gorilla, was unable to do his daily five hours' jousting practice due to the disappearance of his page, Rufus.

Rufus had been sitting in the changing tent, scratching his head, trying to remember the joke somebody once told him, instead of checking Sir Guy's armour for rust, dents, loose bolts and the dreaded armour moth. Meanwhile, his friend and constant companion, Sweep the spaniel, had crawled under Sir Guy's mighty shield and become entangled in its leather straps. When Sweep started hurtling round the tent in a panic, Rufus looked up to see the shield crashing about

MAIN GATE
Last one in please lock up
and put cat out

wildly, and thought he was about to be
attacked by a very cross Giant Smooth-
Backed Tortoise.

Rufus shot out of the tent, through the main
gate (which wasn't open at the time), across
the moat, into the dark forest and up the
tallest tree, where he vowed he would stay for
the rest of his life – or at least until his page's
pension was due.

This page has taken Industrial Action becduse it wants to be the same sort of page as Rufus.

Sweep, being the faithful dog she was, followed Rufus, still wearing the shield, out of the tent, through the main gate (which now has a Rufus-shaped hole in it), across the moat, into the dark forest and up the tree.

"Oh no! It's a Giant Tree-Climbing Smooth-Backed Tortoise!" cried Rufus. He leapt from the top of the tree and landed on a pile of soggy wood-shavings (the life-savings of a woodland peasant). It was only when he saw Sweep drifting down above him, using the shield as a parachute,

AND THIS BEFORE PARACHUTES HAD BEEN INVENTED!

CLEVER KNOW-ALL

that Rufus realised his mistake.

Sir Guy was furious when he heard about this. On the advice of Wizard Wishneck, the Ancient Apothecary, Sir Guy took two snail droppings to calm him down, and retired to bed for the rest of the day.

The next day, following a satisfactory morning's joust, Sir Guy de Gorilla took a quick shower, rubbed himself down and then removed his armour. Refreshed and invigorated, he stretched his arms, stepped forward, slipped on some freshly ironed armour and crashed to the floor. "Rufus!" he cried, "I told you not to leave my armour all over the place for someone to slip on!"

News of the Joke Competition had even reached Sir Guy, who was *very* excited. At last he would have a chance to show off his ancient collection of dragon jokes. Rufus collected up the huge scrolls of parchment and struggled out of the door of his quarters.

...IT WAS LESS OF A STRUGGLE GETTING OUT OF HIS HALVES, AND NO TROUBLE AT ALL GETTING OUT OF HIS WHOLES...

MOUSE WITH RED NOSE (FALSE)

Sir Guy snatched the scrolls impatiently from his page, and, resplendent in his clean glistening armour, clanked, squeaked and crunched his way through the dark echoing corridors of Crumblyn Castle. Sparks flew as his armoured elbows skimmed the rough rock walls. People in his way had to dive into tiny alcoves or doorways as the great pile of metal strode by.

Sir Guy was so excited about his dragon jokes that he couldn't wait for the day of the competition. He burst through the Great Oak

Doors of the Great Crumblyn Hall, without waiting for an anouncement from the Royal Guard. "Your Great Bamboozledness!" he bellowed down the length of the Hall, startling King Boris, who had just that moment nodded off to sleep.

Boris pulled himself up, straightened his ancient crown and looked, blearily, in the direction of Sir Guy.

"It is I, Sire!" boomed Sir Guy.

"Isaiah who?" asked King Boris, thinking that this must be another of those peculiar Knock Knock jokes that he didn't understand.

"No Sire! Sir Guy, Sire!"

King Boris ran the words through his brain several times, then shook his head forlornly so that his crown nearly slipped from his bamboozled bonce.

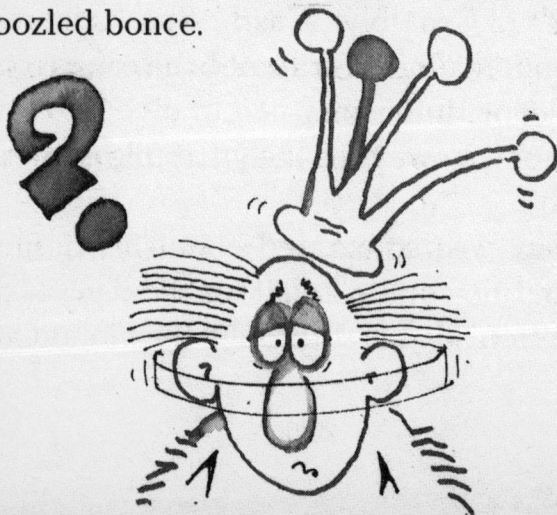

"Nope," he said after a long silence. "Can't see anything funny in that . . ."

The tempestuous Sir Guy sighed in frustration, and stepped forward out of the gloom.

"Your Majesty! It is I! Sir Guy de Gorilla! I come with many jokes to tickle the Royal Funnybone, Sire!"

"Sir Guy! It's you! Have you brought some jokes?"

"Yes Sire!" said Sir Guy, beginning to lose patience with the King.

"Well, I hope they're better than the last lot!"

Sir Guy gritted his teeth, cleared his throat, unrolled the first scroll of dragon jokes and began to read . . .

Name four members of the Dragon family.
Mummy Dragon, Daddy Dragon and two little Dragons.

Why are dragons red and green and scaly?
So you can tell them apart from sheep.

Why are dragons so big and red and green and scaly?
Because if they were small and red and green and smooth they would be Smarties.

What time is it when a dragon sits on a foot-stool?
Time to get another foot-stool.

How can you tell when a dragon's under your bed?
Your nose touches the ceiling.

How can you tell when there are dragons in your gravy?
It's very VERY lumpy.

What's the difference between a dragon and a biscuit?
You can't dunk a dragon in your tea.

What's the difference between a tomato and a white dragon?
The tomato is red.

What do dragons have that no other creature has?
Baby dragons.

What's the difference between a dragon and a flea?
A dragon can have fleas, but a flea can't have dragons.

What would you give a bad-tempered dragon?
Plenty of room.

What does a dragon become after it's one year old?
Two years old.

What do you do if you find a dragon sleeping in your bed?
Sleep somewhere else.

What's red and green and scaly and can't sit down?
A dragon with nappy rash.

What's the same size as a dragon yet weighs nothing at all?
A dragon's shadow.

Why are dragons such terrible dancers?
They have two left feet.

What's the difference between a dragon and a banana?
Have you ever tried peeling a dragon?

"What's the difference between a dragon and a chocolate bar?"
"I don't know."
"Well, I'm not going to send you out to buy some chocolate!"

What's red and green and scaly and squirts jam at you?
A dragon eating a doughnut.

How do you stop a dragon getting through a key-hole?
Tie a knot in its tail.

How can you tell the difference between a dragon and a box of biscuits?
Try lifting it up. If you can't, it's either a dragon or the heaviest box of biscuits in the world.

Click-Click

Everyone in the castle was greatly relieved to hear that the Joke Competition had interrupted Horris, the one-toothed hunchback, who lived in a tiny room at the top of the North Tower. Horris's hobby was knitting. But he didn't just knit anything. No, Horris specialised in baggy swimming costumes in coarse olive-green wool. The wool had been left to him by an uncle who had a vast herd of coarse olive-green sheep. There was so much of it that Horris had enough to knit a lovely green swimming costume for everyone in the Kingdom.

Horris had also promised that once all the swimming costumes were finished, he would begin on matching olive-green scarves to be worn with the costumes when the water was cold.

click-click clickety-click

However, after hearing of the King's decree, Horris actually put down his knitting needles for the first time in 27 years. He then picked up his pen to write down his favourite joke, but then he remembered that he couldn't write. So he put down his pen, picked up his needles and started to knit his favourite joke . . . in coarse olive-green wool, of course.

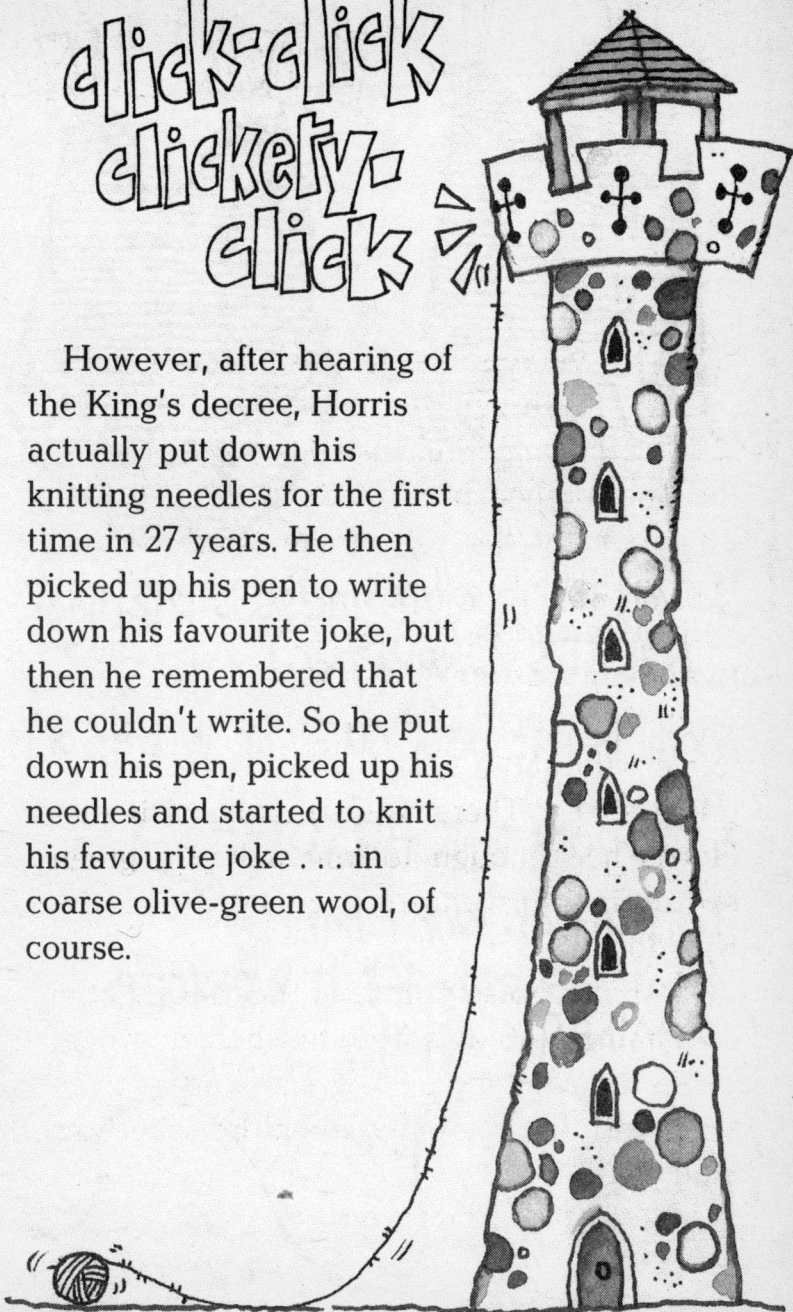

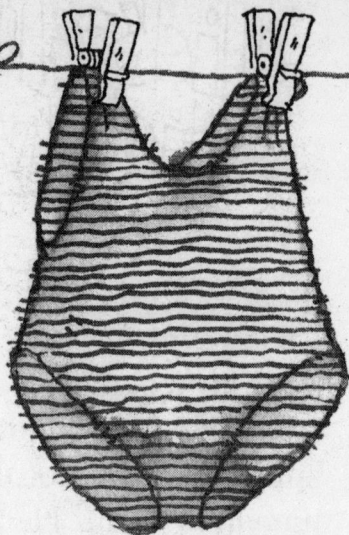

Do you think clumsiness is catching?
NO! IT'S DROPPING!

What is the best cure for water on the brain?
A TAP ON THE HEAD!

This match won't light!
THAT'S STRANGE! IT WORKED A MINUTE AGO!

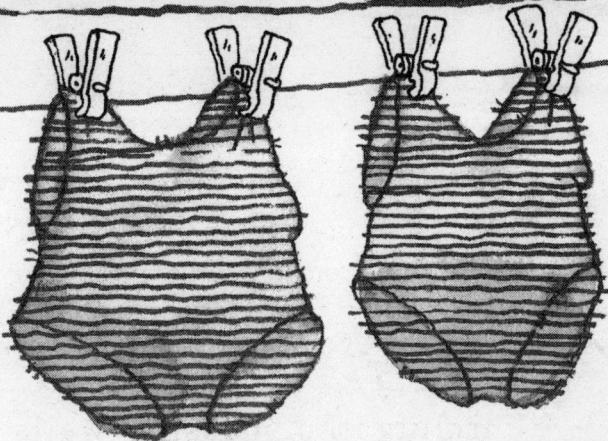

Can you stand on your head?
NO! IT'S TOO HiGH!

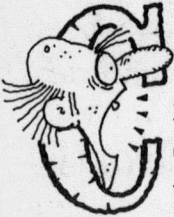

ircling the massive walls of Crumblyn Castle was the greeny-brown water of the moat. A boat-race was held in the moat each year in early spring. At least, it was *called* a race, but the Castle only had one boat, so it wasn't all that exciting to watch. The rest of the year the water just lay there like green gravy.

Two men, Jeeks and Snailbutt, stood up to their necks in the murky water, with half of a large wooden barrel bobbing up and down behind them.

Jeeks and Snailbutt were the latest in a long family line to have the job of dredging the Crumblyn Castle moat. Each summer, all the stagnant mud and rotting weeds would come together to create a stench that smelt rather like a sea of bad eggs. The task had been passed down from father to son for centuries, partly because most members of the family seemed to have extraordinarily long legs (which were useful when standing in the deeper parts of the moat), but mainly because no-one else wanted the job, thank you very much.

Unfortunately, the work meant that even if they had ever taken a bath (and there was no record of such an event) Jeeks and Snailbutt would never *ever* have managed to remove the moaty pong from their persons. As a result, they were forbidden entry to the castle, and had to live deep in the forest, moving hut every time the wind changed direction.

Being keen gossips, but unable to get close enough to anyone to hear any, the family had developed an ingenious method of speaking, for which mere castle walls were no barrier, and ear-plugs worse than useless. It was called "shouting". They were so used to hollering their conversations at friends inside the castle that they had lost the ability to speak normally – even to another family member.

"HAVE YE 'EARD ABOUT THE COMPELI-TITION!?" yelled Jeeks to his partner. Snail-butt was standing right next to him.

"WHAT COMPELITITION!?" he bellowed back, practically biting Jeeks' ear as he spoke.

"THIS 'ERE COMPELITITION O'BOZZ'S!"

(*Note: King Boris was known by all Crumblyners as "Bozz" or "Bozzy" or sometimes "Old Bozzy" but, of course, never to his face, as that would have been the fastest route to the Dragon's breakfast plate.) (*Another note – sorry: Just to say that "Crumblyners" are the people who live in or around Crumblyn Castle, but you probably worked that out already.)

"... I'VE FORGOT WHAT I WAS SAYIN'
NOW!" hollered Jeeks.

"SOMETHIN' ABOUT A COMPELITI-
TION!" shrieked Snailbutt. Jeeks nodded and
got a mouthful of water.

"PHLLLERRRR!" he shouted as he spat out
a fish. "'TIS A COMPELITITION O'JOKES!"
he continued.

"YOU ENTERIN'?" asked Snailbutt.

"YUS! YOU?"

Snailbutt nodded and got a mouthful of
water. "PHLLLERRR!" he spat out the same
fish.

Jeeks and Snailbutt stopped their dredging for a while as they daydreamed about what they would do with all those rocks if they were lucky enough to win the Competition. But dredging was in their blood and it was what they did best, so they agreed loudly to write down any jokes they could think of when they had finished their day's work. And, of course, it's a bit difficult to write down jokes when you're up to your neck in murky water.

"OH WELL! BACK T'WORK!" bellowed Jeeks.

"YUS!" bellowed Snailbutt.

They were trying out a brilliant new idea to make their work much easier. As the water had always been too deep for them to reach the mud in the bottom of the moat, they were trying to devise a way of getting rid of some of the deepest water.

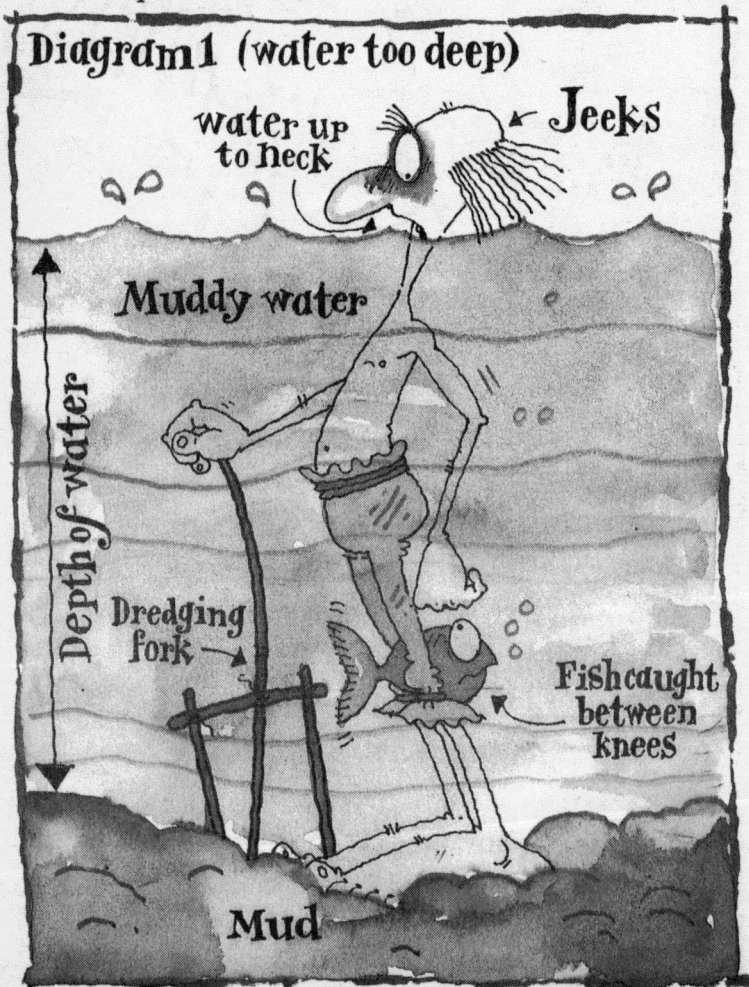

Diagram 1 (water too deep)

water up to neck

Jeeks

Muddy water

Depth of water

Dredging fork →

Fish caught between knees

Mud

Diagram 2 (Jeeks' Plan)

Jeeks fills barrel with deep Moat water

Moat water

Snailbutt drags barrel round to back of moat

Jeeks

Barrel

Snailbutt

Bird's-eye view of Crumblyn Castle and Moat

Jeeks and Snailbutt fill barrel with deep water

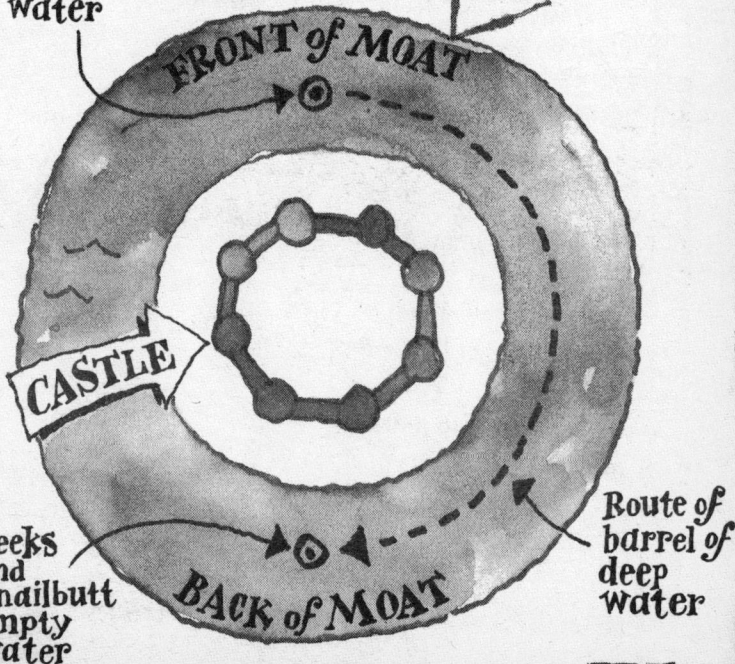

FRONT of MOAT

CASTLE

Jeeks and Snailbutt empty water

BACK of MOAT

Route of barrel of deep water

As the sun went down, the water still hadn't, and they clambered out of the moat, the greeny-brown mud rolling off them in large glistening blobs. "I THINK I KNOW WHAT THE PROBLEM IS . . .!" screamed Jeeks. "WE'LL TRY A BIGGER BARREL TOMORRER!" Snailbutt nodded and they set off, shouting, into the darkness of the forest to compile their list of jokes . . .

Why is the moat so rich?
Because it's got two banks.

What does a deaf fish need?
A herring-aid.

What do you get if you cross a duck with a firework?
A fire-quacker.

What's a frog's favourite food?
A lolli-hop.

What happens when a frog's car breaks down?
It gets toad.

What sort of sheet can't be folded?
A sheet of ice.

What two fish help make a shoe?
A sole and an eel.

Who was the first underwater spy?
James Pond.

What do frogs drink?
Croaka-cola.

What did one fish say to the other fish?
If you keep your mouth shut, you won't get caught.

What's the fastest thing in the water?
A motor-pike.

What's the cleverest fish in the sea?
The brain-sturgeon.

What do you call a baby whale?
A little squirt.

Why are goldfish orange?
The water makes them rusty.

Why was the crab arrested?
Because he kept pinching things.

What fish is famous?
The starfish.

Where do frogs keep their coats?
In the croak-room.

What do you call a frog that's a spy?
A croak and dagger agent.

What do you get if you jump in the Red Sea?
Wet.

At the base of one of the more ricketty castle turrets was a large purple door, which hung awkwardly from the doorpost by a huge buckled hinge. Curious green and pink clouds wafted through the doorway and drifted out into the open air. The clouds were so thick, they almost obscured the weather-beaten notice that was nailed to the door:

OATHS SWORN (& PARDONS BEGG'D)

FURNITURE RECOVER'D

KETTLES DESCAL'D

BOILS LANC'D (we only use Real Lances)

We also cure DRIPPING TAPS ~ and tapping drips

(Available for CHILDREN'S PARTIES)

Inside the tower was a complicated tangle of spiralling tubes, upturned bottles, buckets and old bathtubs, all bubbling and gurgling with brightly coloured liquids. The walls were filled with shelves which sagged under the weight of row upon row of labelled jars.

Through the clouds of swirling green and pink smoke, it was just possible to see two figures sitting on very high stools, busily adjusting their apparatus.

The long, spindly boy hunched up on the lower stool was Pewlingrass, the Wizard's apprentice. Embarrassed by his great height, his back was arched permanently in a huge semi-circle, which made his head droop forward, so that now the tip of his nose was almost touching the swirling potion in front of him.

The Wizard Wishneck occupied the taller stool and was wearing a large pointed hat, in an effort to hide the fact that he was not very tall. A bush of white hair burst from beneath the hat, and a long white beard stretched all the way down to his knees. The Wizard may not have been the tallest person in the kingdom, but he was certainly the oldest – by approximately 103 years, two months, three days, 30 minutes and 42 seconds.

The Wizard grunted and coughed. "Open a

window, Pewlingrass. It's getting a little warm in here," he said in a squeaky voice, as a drifting green cloud enveloped him.

"But . . . but windows haven't been invented yet!" Pewlingrass protested.

"Excuses! It's always excuses with kids today!" mumbled the Wizard into his beard. Nevertheless, he reminded himself to cancel the window cleaner.

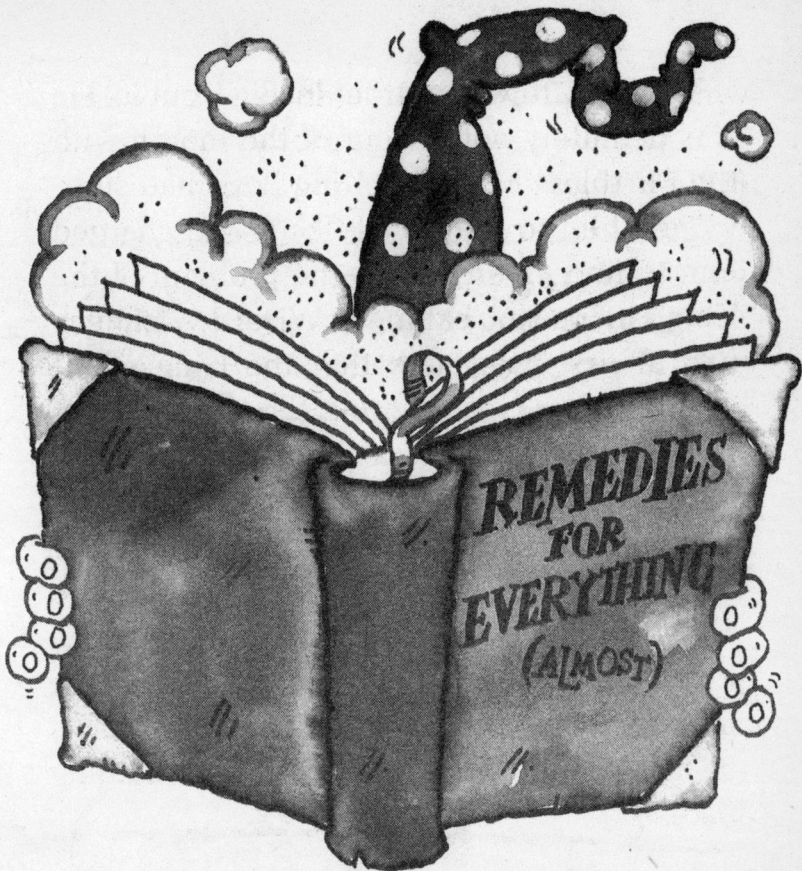

REMEDIES FOR EVERYTHING (ALMOST)

A close look at the Wizard's face (and it would have to be close because of the swirling smoke and the long white hair which covered most of it) would show that he was very worried. He was flicking nervously through a huge dusty book full of strange symbols and diagrams, all the time grunting and squeaking.

The Wizard was in trouble. Big trouble. He was definitely not flavour of the month with the Mirthless Monarch. King Boris had summoned him to the Royal Court and charged him to find an answer to the problem of the King's increasing baldness. Wizard Wishneck had at first suggested that the King might wear a larger crown . . . but the King was not pleased. Then he produced a carefully prepared and hand-tinted clod of moss which he suggested would make a perfect wig. At first this had seemed to be the answer. But, one misty morning, the King took a walk in the Royal Gardens and a light drizzle caused the mossy clod to slither down the back of his neck, leaving a muddy mess on his balding pate.

BOZZ'S
BALDING
BONCE

Eventually, to his great relief, the Wizard Wishneck had come up with a solution. He had managed to concoct a wonder liquid which, within three hours of rubbing into any surface, would grow a thick mat of hair. It even worked when he spilt some on the table. He now had a *very* hairy table.

Unfortunately, he had also been working on a project for the Crumblyn Cricket Club, devising a magic mixture that would give them some lush green grass on their bare and dusty pitch. But somehow, he didn't know how, the labels on the jars had got confused, and he presented the wrong potions to the wrong clients.

It didn't matter too much that the Crumblyn Cricket pitch was now covered in long curly hair (although the CCC were best avoided for a while). But – *oh dear* – a wonderful green lawn, which had to be mowed regularly, had sprung up across the top of Boris's head. The King even had to employ a special Royal Bird-Scarer when he strolled around the Royal Gardens, to stop the birds from searching out worms on his lush green bonce.

The Wizard Wishneck knew that he was Dragon's Dinner if he didn't come up with an antidote soon.

"Are you entering the King's Joke Competition, Master?" asked Apprentice Pewlingrass.

"Joke Competition!" scoffed the Wizard, sifting more and more frantically for possible antidotes through his musty books of magic spells. "Joke Competition! I've got more to think about than some stupid Joke Competition! It's 'Hello Dragon, fancy a bite to eat?' if I don't come up with something pretty soon!"

Then, slowly, he raised his aged head, peered at Pewlingrass through a passing pink cloud, and the tense expression on his hairy face relaxed to reveal the hint of a smile.

The Wizard Wishneck nearly fell off his stool in quivering excitement as Pewlingrass explained the details of the Competition. If only he could make Old Bozzy laugh, the Wizard would be forgiven everything – even the field on Boris's head! He might even tolerate a few daisies!

Wishneck cleared a cob-webby space on his ancient desk, grabbed a buckled old quill pen and some watery brown ink (which was really drinking chocolate, but he didn't notice), and began scratching away at a list of jokes in the back of his *Wizard's Own* diary.

HAZARDOUS VOYAGES by COUNT MEEYOUT

COOKING FOR ONE by Dinah Loan

HOME IMPROVEMENTS by PATTIE O. DAWS

I, A BURGLAR by Robin Banks

BOOM!! by DINAH MYTE

EARTHQUAKE by MAJOR DISASTER

THE HAUNTED HOUSE by Hugo Ferst

TRAINING PARROTS by L.O. POLLY

Tell me, Wise Wizard! What can I do about flat feet?

HAVE YOU TRIED A FOOT PUMP?

How to Cross the Road by LUKE ABOUT

I AM A DEER by Ann T. Lope

THE USELESS HORSEMAN by BETTY PHELLOFF

HOW TO CHEAT AT EXAMS by P. King

SWIMMING TO THE ARCTIC by I.C. WALTERS

A LIFETIME IN BOXING by I.C. Stars

EMBARRASSING MOMENTS BY LUCY LASTICK

WILLIE WIN by Betty Woant

STANDING IN HIGH WINDS by Eileen Nova

SAYING YOUR PRAYERS by Neil Down

Help me, Wise Wizard! Everyone thinks I'm a cricket ball.
How's that?
Not you as well . . .!

Wise Wizard! I keep thinking I'm a ball of string.
Get knotted.

Wise Wizard! No-one takes me seriously.
You must be joking!

Wise Wizard! I keep thinking I'm a dog.
Just lie on the couch and tell me about it.
I can't. I'm not allowed on the furniture.

Help me, Wise Wizard! My father thinks he's a lift.
Tell him to come in.
I can't. He doesn't stop on this floor.

Tell me, Wise Wizard, what do seven days of dieting do?
Make one weak.

Help me, Wise Wizard! I keep telling lies.
I don't believe a word of it.

Tell me, Wise Wizard, can you give me something for my liver?
How about a few onions?

Help me, Wise Wizard. I feel like a bridge.
What's come over you?
A cart and two cows, so far.

Tell me, Wise Wizard. What do you give someone who feels sick?
Plenty of room.

Help me, Wise Wizard. I've lost my dog.
Have you put up a poster?
Don't be daft! My dog can't read!

Help me, Wise Wizard! I'm worried about my figure.
You'll just have to diet.
Yes, but what colour?

KRRRRANNG!

It was an horrendous crash, that sounded as if all the heavy rusting armour in Crumblyn Castle had been dropped from the top of the highest tower. Clouds of startled pigeons leapt into the air from their homes in the nooks and crevices of the castle and a curtain of feathers showered down onto the buildings below.

"By Old Bozzy's Best Bathing Boots!" exclaimed Tully, a castle cleaner, as he dangled halfway down one of the outside walls of the same tower that the noise had come from. "What on *earth* was that?"

PAAAARRRPP!

TOOOOT!

PARRRRPP!

KERPDOIIING!!

"It's band-practice time!" yelled Tully's colleague, as he dangled from the other side of the tower. Yes, it was Thursday at 7.33 in the morning – the traditional time for the Royal Crumblyn Musyke-Masters Orchestra and Choir to start their weekly rehearsal. Their conductor was the distinguished Dame Brenda Bazoon, who had been given her dameship for bird-scaring services to the castle.

SHARP

BLUNT

Loudo

Dame Brenda had composed a new anthem in honour of King Boris, and was sure that this one would prove even more popular than the previous forty-three. It was called *"Hail to Our Beloved King Boris Who Brightens Our Lives with his Ready Wit, Sparkling Sense of Humour and Endless Collection of Hilarious*

Jokes and Stories". She had great hopes for it in the forthcoming Joke Competition. Her last offering, "*King Boris is an Alright Kinda Guy, Right On!*" she had decided was probably a bit ahead of its time, and the one before that, "*Very Flattering Anthem for King Boris*", was perhaps a little too obvious.

But this rehearsal had not started well. Some members of the orchestra hadn't started at all, while others had started too soon and the choir had started in a different key.

Dame Brenda bounced up and down on her podium, waving her arms to stop the orchestra. But the faster and more furiously she waved, the faster and more furiously they played and sang. Giant drums boomed, voices soared, cymbals crashed, gongs gonged, curious

bowed instruments scraped and squealed, and long and short, fat, thin and curly wooden tubes tooted and blasted, squeaked and groaned. Odd bits of gargoyle, rock and slate tumbled from the tower walls as the orchestra and choir approached breakneck speed. The whole tower began to vibrate, and the two cleaners dangling from their ropes outside walls hurriedly lowered themselves to the ground and raced through the crashing masonry to safety.

Eventually, Dame Brenda decided to let the piece run its course. She swept off her podium and retreated into a small room specially reserved for sulking artistic geniuses. There she lay down to wait for the Anthem to finish. Slowly, the racket subsided as the instruments came one by one to the end. Finally, all that was left was the tinny sound of a solitary oboe, tweeting its lonely way to the finish.

Then there was silence – apart from the thump and crunch of odd lumps of masonry that were still dislodging themselves from above.

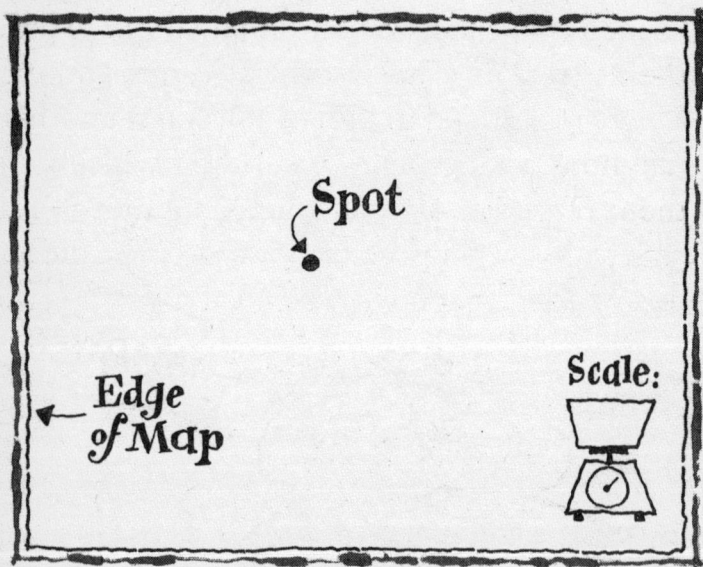

MAP

After spending a short time re-composing herself, Dame Brenda stepped out again onto her podium, crunching over pieces of plaster that had fallen from the walls and ceiling. The orchestra and choir, all covered in plaster and dust, were excitedly congratulating themselves on a brilliant performance. Until, that is, they saw Dame Brenda's furious face and the big black cloud, with streaks of lightning flashing out of it, which hovered over her head.

All went quiet, and the musicians pretended to be studying their music, whilst Dame Brenda spent half an hour telling them to pull their socks up. (Those with socks did, and the others pretended to.) Then she spent another half hour telling them to get their wits about them. (This was difficult enough for those with wits to do, but impossible for those who didn't even know what a wit was.)

Suitably ticked-off, the orchestra and choir were ready for another attempt at the great Anthem. Dame Brenda raised her baton high in the air, then swung it into action energetically, shouting "Go, my children!"

The orchestra plunged into the piece once again, but this time they all started together. The first massive chord produced a billowing cloud of white dust from the masonry above, whilst outside another rock crashed to the ground.

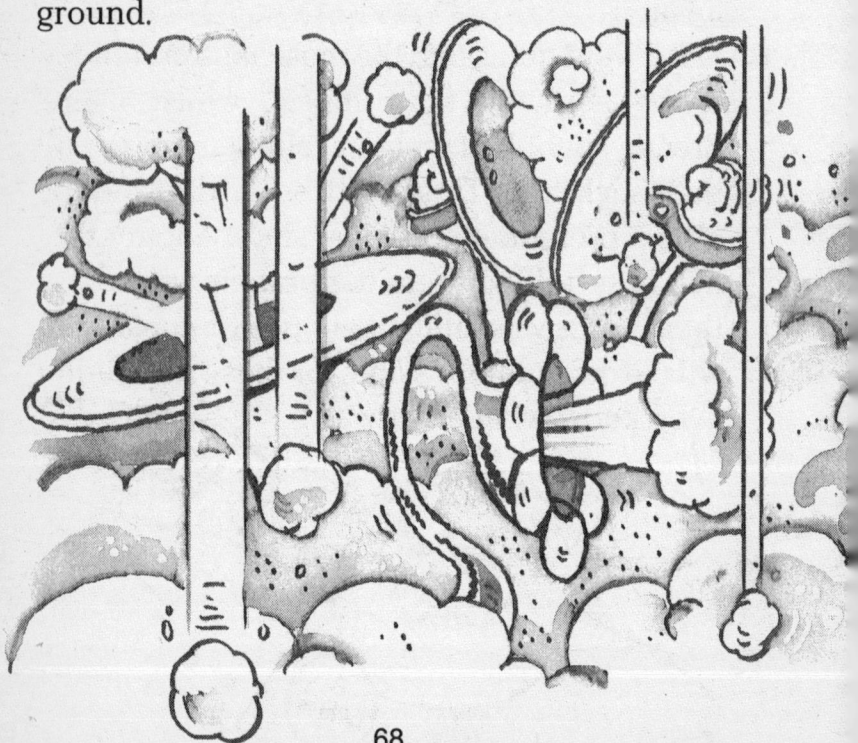

The orchestra played on, the choir sang on, with Dame Brenda swinging her arms wildly, transported by her own composition. Neither she nor the orchestra or choir noticed what was happening around them. A thickening layer of plaster was gradually settling on each musician, until at last the ensemble seemed to have disappeared completely under a huge fall of snow.

But still they played on. Larger lumps of masonry rained down on them, and more rocks and slates scattered the ground outside. Holes began to appear in the walls, and patches of sky could be seen through the roof. A piece of rock fell right into the bell of one musician's tuba, making him produce a noise like a startled horse. With one great blast he managed to expel the rock like a giant pea-shooter, and it flew through the air, narrowly missing Dame Brenda, and shot a further hole in the disintegrating wall.

The structure of the tower began to creak as the music got louder. The beams which held up the roof folded, so that above them was only sky. Strings began to snap on the bowed instruments. The woodwind instruments puffed out clouds of plaster like smoke signals.

Lumps of masonry bounced off the drums with a loud

BOOOYYYYOOOiiiiNNNGG!!

and spiralled back into the air, sometimes splitting into smaller pieces like a strange sort of dusty firework display.

But the musicians played on. The wind began to gust through the gaps in the walls, swirling up the dust of the plaster. Whole slabs of wall began to keel over and tumble away. Down below (at a safe distance) an amazed crowd gathered to watch the peculiar spectacle. Totally exposed, with all the top flight of the tower gone, the orchestra and choir were silhouetted against the sky, whilst the bouncing figure of Dame Brenda still conducted furiously.

Rocks from lower down the tower began to loosen and drop – small ones at first, then larger ones.

Dame Brenda Bazoon drove her musicians dramatically towards the last bar, and with a final flourish the choir and orchestra stopped . . . and all together too!

"Well done, my children! Well *done!*" she enthused, exhausted but happy. She looked around her at the swirling dusty wasteland, then at the amazed faces way below on the ground, then at where the walls weren't, and then at where the roof wasn't . . .

"Run for it!" she hollered, flinging her baton into the air and making for the steps that, luckily, still spiralled down the side of what was left of the tower. The orchestra and choir hurried after her. Loud booming, crunching, twanging and clanging sounds accompanied them, as feet went through drum skins, wind instruments were crushed, strings were snapped and cymbals were buckled.

Dame Brenda burst out into the courtyard, with the others right behind her, just in time to see the lower walls of the tower split open, floor by floor, and crash to the ground in an all-enveloping cloud of dust.

Everyone stared, blinking, as the dust settled. The tower had completely disappeared, leaving just a pile of rubble.

"Oh dear," muttered a bass drummer nervously. "Er, anyone know any brilliant jokes?"

Where would you get a job playing a rubber trumpet?
In an elastic band.

Why do so few people play the harp?
Because it takes a lot of pluck.

What kind of sugar sings?
Icing sugar.

What's the difference between a fish and a piano?
You can't tuna fish.

What dance do ducks do?
The quackstep.

What instrument does a fish play?
The bass guitar.

Which part of your body can you play?
The trombone.

Which other part of your body can you play?
The tri-ankle.

Buttriss was a big man. A very big man. No, even bigger than that – a VERY big man. He was so heavy that he wasn't allowed to go above the ground floor of the castle for fear of damaging its ricketty structure. (He couldn't get through most of the doors anyway) Many Crumblyners were sure that even Foigle, the fierce and frightening dragon, was terrified of him – but no-one had actually bothered to ask the dragon.

In fact, Buttriss had loved all animals, whether they were big, medium-sized or small, from as far back as he could remember. All he had cared about was animals, ever since he had nursed a confused and lonely woodlouse, called Reginald, back to health and happiness. He had found Reginald as a stray wandering aimlessly around the castle grounds, hungry and friendless, and had fed him, taken him for walks on a tiny lead, and tucked him up in bed each night with a little story about woodlouse folk (after giving him a good wash and cleaning his teeth, of course, because a woodlouse can get very dirty being so close to the ground all the time).

I LOVE MY UNCLE BUTTRISS!

Eventually, Reginald got married and had a huge family, but he never forgot Buttriss, and still sends him a card every year on his birthday. The family always look forward to visiting "Uncle" Buttriss.

As Buttriss grew up (and up and up and up) he found more animals to adopt or care for. He spent long hours working on fantastic inventions to make their little lives easier. First there was the "belly wheel" he made for a dachshund to stop its belly scraping on the ground when it walked . . .

then the tiny doorbell he designed for a snail when it was inside its shell . . .

PLEASE RING

then the battery-driven heated egg-cosies he invented for the chickens so that they wouldn't have to spend all their time sitting on the eggs . . .

CHICKEN TIMES

CHICKEN BATTERY

and the special fire-extinguisher he left in the forest for the Dragon – just in case he had an accident with his fiery breath . . .

Buttriss *cared*. He cared *so* much that he would climb trees to rescue birds if he thought they were stuck, and he would bore little holes in the ground so that worms wouldn't bruise their noses when they tunnelled.

But his main love was horses. He would do *anything* for horses. His idea of taking a horse for a gallop was to race round the outside of the castle with the horse in his arms. The horse would feel better for a spot of fresh air and change of scenery, yet not too exhausted or sweaty. In fact, the horse would often ask to be taken round the castle again, or perhaps a little farther afield if it was a nice day, with sometimes a spot of fence-jumping for a bit of excitement. And Buttriss was always ready to oblige. After a day's galloping and cantering, he would cook them all a delicious supper, put each horse to bed (in beds that he had designed and made specially), and sing them lullabies until their tired little eyelids flickered and closed.

The next morning he would bring them each breakfast in bed with a copy of *Horse Daily* or *Stable Fun*, and always let them have a lie-in if they felt they needed one.

But Buttriss had one *big* problem. King Boris had complained about the clattering of the horses' hooves (when Buttriss wasn't carrying them). It was true that they *did* make a noise on the Crumblyn Castle flag-stones, and the sound *did* echo loudly around the walls of the castle.

Eventually, a Royal Dictum had been brought down by King Boris's Royal Dictum Deliverer, which told Buttriss that if the horses' hooves continued to disturb the Royal Snooze, the horses would have to go. No ifs, buts or maybes – if King Boris said something, that was IT … (If King Boris said *anything*, that was IT!)

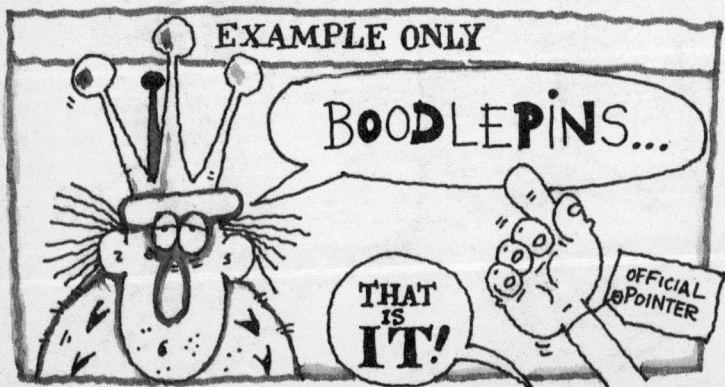

Buttriss sat up all night, trying to think up a solution, but eventually he fell into a fitful sleep, only to be woken the next morning by the sound of the horses complaining from their beds that they hadn't had their breakfasts and comics delivered.

He staggered blearily out of bed and put on his huge slippers . . . then he had his idea! Slippers! Horse Slippers! They would stop all the noise! After sorting out all the breakfasts and comics, he sat down to make all his horses a set of slippers each. This took him most of the day, but the horses didn't mind staying in bed because they had their colour supplements to catch up on.

ALMOST SILENCE

They were *wonderful* slippers! Each horse had a different colour, and on the front of each slipper was a fluffy white bunny. The horses loved them! They jumped from their beds, slipped them on and couldn't wait to try them out. They all queued up at the castle gate (almost silently!), and, without waiting for the drawbridge to be lowered, leapt noiselessly across the moat and galloped quietly round and round the castle, happily showing off their brand-new slippers.

Buttriss stood and watched. A broad smile stretched across his face, from ear to ear. After a few circuits of the castle, his horses romped into the forest beyond, and disappeared off through the trees.

With mingling tears of joy and sadness, Buttriss realized that he now had nothing to do. But as he turned to wend his weary way home alone, he spotted King Boris's decree nailed to the castle wall.

"Animal jokes!" he squeaked to himself excitedly. "King Boris'll die laughing when he hears my brilliant collection of animal jokes!"

Why was the centipede late for the football match?
He was putting his boots on.

What animal wears a fur coat in the winter and pants in the summer?
A dog.

Why aren't elephants allowed on the beach?
Their trunks might fall down.

Why is a snake so smart?
You can't pull its leg.

What kind of tie does a pig wear?
A pigsty.

Why couldn't the two elephants go into the water?
They only had one pair of trunks between them.

Why can't you have a conversation with a goat around?
Because it keeps butting in.

Why do cats turn round and round before sleeping?
Because one good turn deserves another.

What do you call a monkey with a crossbow?
Sir.

What is cowhide most used for?
Holding cows together.

What do you get if you pour boiling water down rabbit holes?
Hot cross bunnies.

What do you get if you cross a hedgehog with a giraffe?

A 3-METRE TOOTHBRUSH!

What time is it when you meet a crocodile?

TIME TO RUN!

Buttriss tries a new hare-do...

oooooooooooh! Aren't they *PRETTY*!"
Princess Nausea squealed as she
sat on her bejewelled stool. Two
handmaidens were plaiting her long red hair.
"Yes Ma'am," they answered, not bothering
to look at whatever it was she was squealing
about.

The Princess was in fact gazing at the vast
display of gems, trinkets and ornaments that
were crowded onto every available space in
her luxury chambers.

"Ooooooh! Aren't they *gorgeous*!" The
Princess was a keen collector. She had started
by collecting priceless diamonds and pearls,
necklaces and rings, but now she collected
everything she could lay her hands on,
including ear plugs, shoe buckles, old pieces
of toast and even tumblers full of dirt.

"Oooooooooooh!" she squealed again.

"Yes Ma'am," said the handmaidens.

"I haven't asked you anything yet!" she scolded.

"Yes Ma'am," they said again.

CRUMBLYN

"Oooooooohh! Isn't it *lovely*!" the Princess went on. Then, suddenly she jumped up to grab and kiss one of her ornaments. A handmaiden shot after her. (She had plaited her thumb into the Princess's hair.) Princess Nausea shook a little model of Crumblyn Castle in a glass dome and watched it rain.

"Ooooooooooh!" she cried disappointedly. "It's supposed to snow!"

"Yes Ma'am, perhaps it's the warmer weather," said the handmaiden with the thumb in her hair. But the Princess wasn't listening. She wandered back to her stool and lifted her mirror.

"Do my hair again," she commanded.

"Yes Ma'am," said the two handmaidens, who pretended to start again by flapping their hands about fussily.

"Ooooooooooh!" said the Princess, not in her "Isn't it *pretty*!" voice, but in her "Golly, that's a surprise!" voice.

The two handmaidens were relieved to hear something different and looked up, then looked at each other and shrugged their shoulders. They couldn't see anything.

"Loooooooook!" she cried in her "I'm still surprised!" voice, and pointed to the window. There, puffing and panting on the window ledge was a little fat green frog.

"Isn't it *pretty*!" exclaimed the Princess.

"Y . . . yes Ma'am," said the handmaidens, suspiciously.

"Great Piles of Pondweed!" gasped the little frog. "That was some climb!"

"Oooooooooh!" squealed Princess Nausea. "It can talk!"

"I can talk better than I can climb, these days," said the frog gruffly, wiping its brow. "You don't have a goblet of water, do you?"

The Princess waved her hand and a handmaiden went off to fetch some water. With a – PALLOPP! – the frog jumped straight into it.

"Ahhh! That's better! It's a bit too warm this time of year for frogs to go climbing towers," it sighed.

"Have you really just climbed all the way up the outside of this tower?" asked the Princess in her very high voice, and blinking in disbelief. (They were on the twelfth floor.)

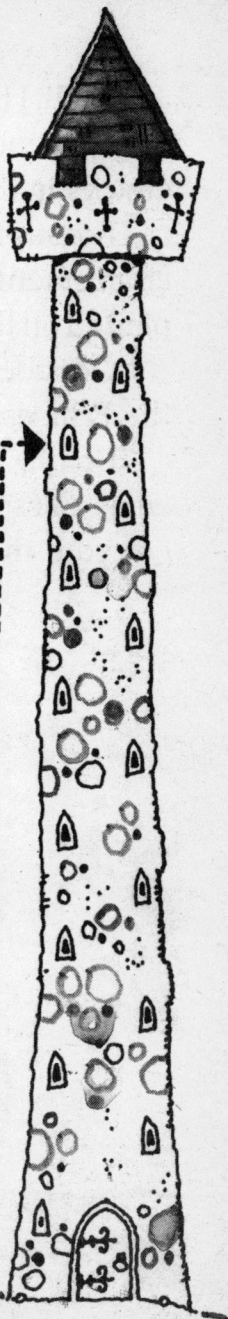

FROG ROUTE

"Well, I hardly flew here, did I!" scoffed the frog, lolling in the water and flapping his elbows in a mock-flying motion.

The handmaidens, staring in open-mouthed amazement at this talking frog, had now plaited all their fingers into the Princess's hair.

"Ooooooooohh! Isn't he *super*!" screeched the Princess.

"Uh uh," said the two handmaidens. (This is what "Yes Ma'am" sounds like when you've got your mouth wide open in amazement.)

The frog, seeing that some explanation was called for, began his story. "My name is Martin, and I'm a Prince–" a gale of laughter stopped his flow. "No! Really!" he insisted, sounding slightly hurt. But the three maidens weren't listening. They were too busy struggling to catch their breath, as they gasped and screeched with laughter.

"Sorry . . . Martin!" said the Princess after some minutes, red-faced and trying to pull herself together. "You were saying?" she squeaked, holding her hand over her mouth to stop another explosion of laughter.

Gritting what would be his teeth, if frogs had any teeth, he continued. "I come from a land many many miles away from here. I have

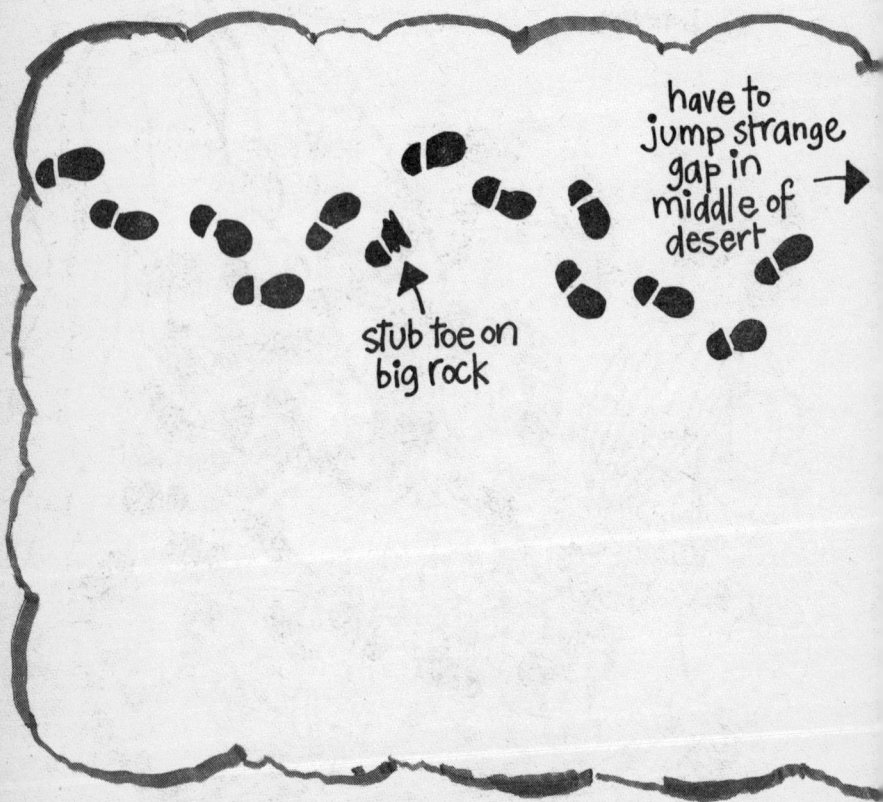

have to jump strange gap in middle of desert →

stub toe on big rock

"...Just a small part of my Heroic Trek across

travelled both by night and by day. I have grappled with wicked knights, had fierce arguments with evil giants and some very strong differences of opinion with bad-tempered dragons. I have scaled sheer cliffs, trekked barren deserts and frozen wastelands and swum raging torrents, risking my life every step of the way, and got two blisters..."

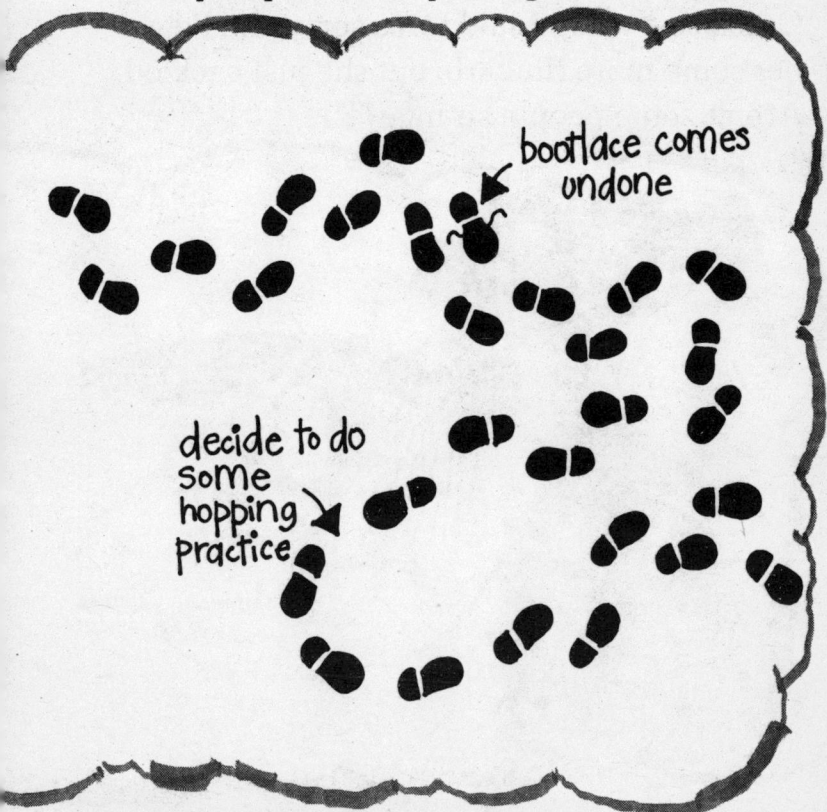

bootlace comes undone

decide to do some hopping practice

a particularly barren desert..."

"Ooooooooooh!" squealed the three maidens.

". . . Then," Martin continued, pulling himself up over the side of the goblet, lurching towards his audience, and jumping up and down with excitement, "I came across an old hag with a long lumpy nose and a black pointy hat. When I accidentally walked over her rhubarb patch, she turned me into a frog! Quick as a wink I said I was sorry and I'd get her some more rhubarb, but she just cackled. Aren't some people strange?"

...."I have a difference of opinion with

The three maidens found themselves nodding, fascinated. "Now the thing is . . . and this is where I think you can help, Princess . . . this old witch – you'll love this! – this old witch said that the only way that I can get out of being a frog is if – and this is the crux of it, basically – if someone . . . *hrmmp!* . . . someone of your station, so to speak, you know, being a Princess and so-forth. . . ."

"Oh! Get on with it!" snapped the Princess.

an elderly gardener . . ."

"Yes! Quite! So anyway . . . if you don't mind . . . and I'd be really grateful and suchlike . . . what's required is . . . hrmmmp! . . ." Have you ever seen a frog blush? This one did!

This picture is for the benefit of those with black-and-white books:

DEEP RED

DEEP RED

The Princess was getting very irritated. "Get on with it, Frogs-spawn brain!"

"Sorry, yes . . . it's a little tricky, you see . . . what's needed is . . . a little kiss . . . sort of . . ."

The Princess stared at the frog, and the frog looked anywhere but at the Princess. "A *kiss*?!" she squealed. "Me kiss a *frog*!? What kind of a Princess do you think I am? What would everyone say?!"

"W . . . would they have to know?" the frog suggested, timidly.

"*I'd* know!" objected Princess Nausea, and she stormed off to her bedroom, quickly followed by her two handmaidens (who still had their fingers plaited into her hair).

The frog looked sadly over the top of the goblet.

"He *is* a Prince, Ma'am!" whispered one handmaiden.

"No he's not! He's a *frog!*" snarled the Princess, with the expression of someone who had just had her face pushed inside-out.

"What would be nice, though," she thought aloud, "would be if I could keep the little frog with my other ornaments . . ."

The handmaidens laughed. "It would never be able to sit still long enough!" said one.

"Or sit still without saying something!" said the other.

Princess Nausea smiled. "Run and find the Wizard Wishneck immediately," she said, "and get him to give you a small bottle of his Patent Pebble Potion! Run!"

The handmaidens disentangled their fingers from the Princess's hair, and ran.

An hour and seven minutes later, a handmaiden reappeared, gasping for breath and clutching the potion in her hand.

Actually, the potion was invented by the Wizard Wishneck after the Princess had found some tummy-button fluff, and wanted to keep it as an ornament. With just one drop of the potion the fluff had turned to a pebble. Now read on...

CLEVER KNOW-ALL

The Princess swept back to where the little frog still lolled, exhausted, in the goblet. She sprinkled two drops of the potion in the water and the frog was turned to stone.

Proudly, Princess Nausea positioned her new ornament in front of all the other gems, diamonds, trinkets, lollipop sticks and souvenirs.

"Isn't it *pretty?*" she squealed.

"Yes Ma'am," chorused the two hand-maidens.

But it wasn't long before she was bored with her new ornament. Not having anything better to do, she started her entry for Daddy's Joke Competition. "I could win a pretty new rock *every* day!" she squealed, and she started to scribble down her list of jokes . . .

What goes in pink and comes out blue?
A SWIMMER ON A COLD DAY!

Will you remember me tomorrow?
OF COURSE!
Will you remember me the day after?
YES, OF COURSE!
Will you remember me the day after that?
CERTAINLY!!
Knock, knock!
WHO'S THERE?
You see! You've forgotten me already!

What did the big candle say to the
little candle?
I'M GOING OUT TONIGHT!

Why did the man sleep with a ruler?
HE WANTED TO SEE HOW LONG
HE SLEPT!

OOOOOOOOOOOOOOOOOOOOOOOOOOOOH!
They're so Funneeee!

he Great Day arrived. All around the Castle Crumblyners were wearing their "Well, It Makes Me Laugh Anyway!" badges and their "If It's Good Enough For King Boris, It's Far Too Good for the Likes of Me!" caps, as they filed into the Great Hall, eager to find out who would win the Great Joke Competition.

GRRRRRR!!

Security was tight, and only those who knew the official password were allowed in. But because the official password was "Let me in", most people were able to get in without too much difficulty. Even the driving rain outside was not enough to dampen their spirits – although it dampened almost everything else, thanks to the number of holes in the roof.

The Royal Crumblyn Musyke-Masters (or the Demolition Team, as the Crumblyners now called them) kept the audience entertained, not so much with the beauty of their music, as with the way the music made every object in the Hall vibrate and dance about.

Wizard Wishneck's
PATENT
ICE CREAM
'Will not melt on your clothes'

The Wizard Wishneck had invented what he called "Ice Cream", which was being sold at a small kiosk just outside the Hall. But it wasn't proving too popular. All he had done, in fact, was to add a few drops of his Patent Pebble Potion into some goblets of milk, so that, however hard you licked, the "Ice Cream" stayed where it was. It was also quite warm. Even holding a flaming torch underneath it wouldn't melt it. (One or two of the Wizard's customers suggested, as they rested their exhausted tongues, that they should hold a flaming torch under the Wizard Wishneck!)

Also on display was a demonstration of close-formation flying by a flock of chickens specially trained for the occasion by Buttriss.

There was a juggler who juggled with large rocks – not the Prize Rocks of course, just very clever replicas; some sheep-dog trials, where the winner was the dog who could do the best impression of a sheep; and a piano-eating contest.

At the North end of the Great Hall, mounted on a dais, was the King's magnificent new throne. He had commanded the Royal Furniture Maker to construct it because the old one, which was made of stone, was bruising the Royal Bottom. This new chair, the Original Crumblyn *Recliner-Throne* as it was called, was a totally new design using up-to-the-minute technology. Jewel-encrusted levers, pulleys and cranks made it possible to move almost every part of the throne in any direction *"for the sitter's maximum comfort and enjoyment"* – as the label said.

A DIMBY
(Artist's Impression)

As befitted a King, the Throne was rich in ornamental carving and thickly upholstered in finest Dimby fur. (This is the skin of the now-extinct Faintly-Spotted High-Backed Dimby, that used to roam the plains near Crumblyn Castle. It was a chair-shaped animal with four stiff legs.)

Above the Throne was the apparatus designed to show the audience which (if any) of the jokes the King could understand. It was a long plank, painted in Crumblyn yellow, on which the words "We Are Not Amused" were painted. The word "Not" was on a removable flap, to be taken off by an ornately dressed courtier in the event of a titter from the King.

To the sound of a fanfare tweeted by six canaries (also trained by Buttriss) Sir Myles of Tarmac stepped onto the dais and pompously announced the purpose of the occasion. But the audience was restless. "We know all that!" they cried and they continued their excited chatter.

Then, with a flash of Dame Brenda Bazoon's baton, the orchestra burst into life once more, with the opening chords of King Boris's Anthem. As small pieces of soggy plaster drifted down from above, the slight figure of King Boris the Bamboozled appeared, with his crown strapped firmly under his chin just in case he dozed off during the proceedings. Sir Myles ushered King Boris to his new throne, and Boris relaxed into it sleepily.

The Anthem was over, the structure of the Great Hall was, amazingly, more or less intact and the Competition proper was about to begin. Sir Myles took up a huge scroll and began to read the joke entries that had been copied out by the Crumblyn scribes. At each joke guffaws and titters would break forth from the crowd. Some Crumblyners would even roll about in the aisles – their laughter completely beyond control. Then, as the audience calmed down, all eyes would turn towards the King. But his bored face never cracked into a smile. He just sank deeper and deeper into his comfortable new throne, and his eyelids grew heavier. Sometimes he sat up at the end of a joke, and the audience, with tears of laughter sparkling in their eyes, would hold their breath in anticipation.

IS HE GOING TO LAUGH..?
HAS HE FOUND A JOKE HE CAN UNDERSTAND..?
IS THERE ANYTHING UNDER THAT CROWN...?

But then he would just stare into space, shake his head forlornly, say "No . . . don't get it . . ." and sink back into the depths of his throne.

The evening wore on without a titter from the King. Knee-deep in discarded scrolls of jokes, Sir Myles's voice was getting hoarse. The courtier who stood by the "We Are Not Amused" board had lost his official poise and

was slowly sliding down the wall. King Boris occasionally muttered to himself as if he was dreaming, but then fiddled with some of the levers on his throne and moved to a more comfortable position.

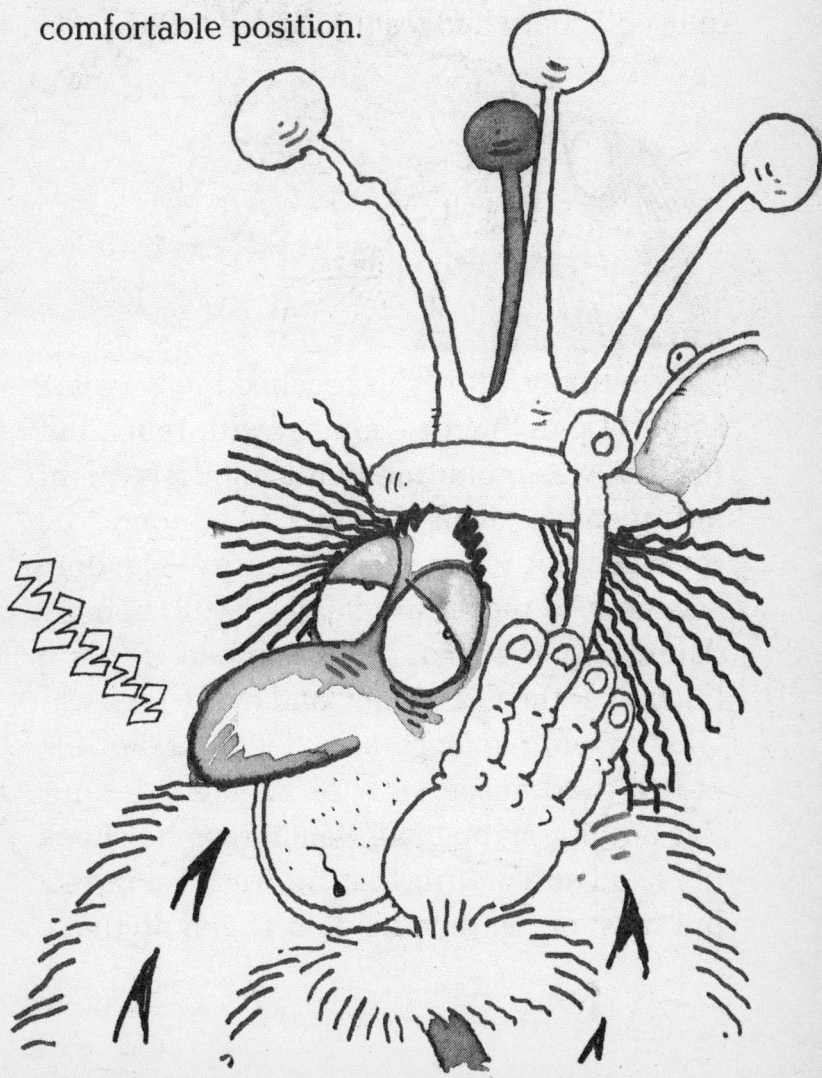

Many disappointed people in the audience saw their chances of winning the life-time's supply of rocks pass them by.

Eventually, Sir Myles reached the very last scroll of parchment – almost with relief. But the fear was mounting that King Boris might not manage even a smile. And once he realized that no-one in the entire Kingdom was able to make him laugh – well, nobody dared to guess what might happen. Tension hung over the Great Hall, and every joke was greeted with exaggerated laughter, as the crowd tried desperately to inspire the King. But nothing happened. Sometimes he shook his head to confirm that he wasn't amused, but most of the time he didn't even do that.

Boris was barely listening to Sir Myles's croakings as he groped to adjust his *Recliner Throne*. He was trying to lower the back and lift up the leg rest slightly. Eventually he found a lever and yanked at it, but with a dreadful KADDDOYYYYNNNGGG!!! and a WHHHIIRRRRR!!! the Throne suddenly changed shape, and the audience gasped with horror as they saw their King's legs fly into the air and he was swallowed into the depths of the chair.

The crowd stood in stunned silence . . . fearing a Very Bad-Tempered King when he had been prised free. Sir Myles and some other courtiers rushed round the throne in a blind panic.

"Sire! Sire! Are you in there?" cried Sir Myles, trying to lever the furniture open. (The Royal Furniture Maker was by this time out of the hall, bags packed, across the drawbridge and into the forest with a new name and false nose.)

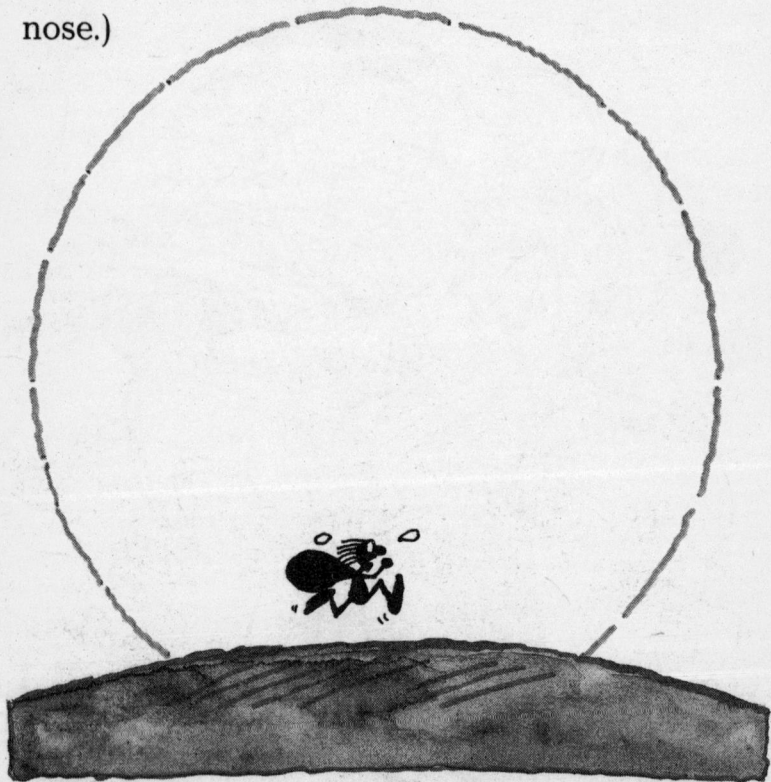

For some time the only sound that could be heard was the chewing of nails as the crowd stood dumb-struck and rooted to the spot. Then, from within the depths of the folded Throne they heard a faint noise . . . It sounded like someone was crying . . . The King's little legs started flapping in the air . . . the Throne began to vibrate slightly and the muffled wailing sound continued . . . They had never heard such a noise coming from their King . . .

It got louder and louder . . . .The Throne shook more . . .The legs flapped more . . .The stuttering noise became louder and louder, broken only by deep intakes of breath . . . He was LAUGHING!

THE KING WAS LAUGHING!

Slowly the crowd relaxed and joined in, until the whole Hall was filled with useless bodies rolling about in helpless laughter. With eyes streaming, the King's Guard managed to force the folded Throne open, to extract a breathless, red-faced, hooting King Boris. He was laughing so much that he had to be held up. Tears gushed down his face, his knees buckled and his crown slipped round the side of his head.

Well, of course, no-one qualified for the prize (apart, perhaps, from the Royal Furniture Maker, but he was never heard of again), so King Boris was able to keep all his rocks, stones and grit. But nobody seemed to mind too much. At last they had a King with a sense of humour . . .

If you like to laugh, you'll be howling for hours with HIPPO's hilarious selection of joke books . . .

Kids' Best Jokes   *Compiled by Karen King*
Long jokes, short jokes, fat jokes, thin jokes . . . they're all shapes and sizes in *Kids' Best Jokes*. But something all these jokes do have in common is that each one is somebody's favourite!   £1.75

The School Joke Book   *Susannah Bradley*
Here's a joke book with a difference. It's huge and it's full of pictures! There's a joke for every school occasion - in the classroom, in the cloakroom, in the toilets, behind the bike sheds . . . - and they're all told by a bunch of crazy cartoon kids! Even the most boring teacher will roar with laughter! £2.50

The Cops 'n' Robbers Joke Book
                    Laura Norder
Did you ever read a joke book with a police siren on the top? Well, now's your chance . . .
    Follow the antics of Burglar Bill, Smasher Smith and Sneaky Sid as they try to escape the clutches of Detective Golightly, P.C. Pouncer and W.P.C. Perfect (not forgetting Woofer the police dog).   £1.75

Father Christmas' Joke Book   *Terry Deary*
At last, Father Christmas has put pen to paper and, with the help of his seven gnomes, he tells you just what Christmas is *really* like at the North Pole (whilst the gnomes tell you just what Father Christmas is *really* like!). Then there are gnome jokes, gnock, gnock jokes, cracker jokes and lots lots more, to make sure this Christmas is truly crazy!   £1.75

Hippo Books publishes poetry too . . .

Book of Beasts *Compiled by Julia Middleton*
You'll find a jungle of beasts prowling through the
pages of this fascinating collection of animal
poems. There are tigers, baboons, yaks, unicorns
and even a duck-billed platypus in a menagerie of
poems by a whole range of poets, including Ted
Hughes, Hilaire Belloc, T S Elliot, Edward Lear
and Spike Milligan. £1.95

The Hippo Book of Hilarious Poetry
Compiled by Terry Deary
Take a plunge into this hilarious collection of
funny verse, and you'll be laughing for hours.
There are silly poems, rude rhymes and all sorts of
ridiculous verses by poets old and new, including
Roald Dahl, Spike Milligan, Ogden Nash and lots
lots more! £1.95